THE
Archive Photographs
SERIES
AROUND
HIGH WYCOMBE

THE
Archive Photographs
SERIES
AROUND
HIGH WYCOMBE

Compiled by
Dennis Edwards

CHALFORD

The Chalford Publishing Company
St Mary's Mill, Chalford,
Stroud, Gloucestershire, GL6 8NX

ISBN 0 7524 1013 X

Typesetting and origination by
The Chalford Publishing Company
Printed in Great Britain by
Bailey Print, Dursley, Gloucestershire

Crendon Street as it looked before it was widened. Christ Church was designed by Henry Vernon and built between 1889/97. The shop on the corner at this time was the local branch of W.H. Smith.

Contents

Introduction

'Sequestered little spot! Adorned by nature with many delightful varieties of hill and dale, it seems to afford security for retirement; and those who love to watch the sparkling brook, and gaze with delight on the verdure and fertility of the surrounding pasture, in preference to luxury; or repose in the shade of the secluded woods, rather than seek the honours of princes, or the equinoctial hurricanes of political notoriety, may dwell for a time in Wycombe . . .'

(Henry Kingston, 1848)

It is almost fifty years since I first visited High Wycombe. I arrived at the railway station in a train of creaking wooden ex-LNER carriages behind a steam locomotive. As the train came to a halt, the ground shook as an express train bound for Paddington thundered through on the fast line.

In the bay platform stood an antique-looking auto-carriage and bubbling tank engine, waiting in vain for the unlikely event of any passengers intending to board it for the trip down the Wye Valley to Bourne End and Maidenhead. In the station yard stood red and cream Thames Valley buses, whilst one of the dark green double-decker London Country buses came down Amersham Hill.

Wycombe seemed so different from the Middlesex suburbs left behind only half an hour before. Here was a busy provincial town, a bustling market and people who spoke with country accents. And between the ancient buildings, one caught sight of the wooded green slopes of the Chiltern Hills.

Times have changed. Although Wycombe escaped the worst ravages of the 1960s, the developers of the last decade and the need for traffic relief systems, have swept away a great deal of the old town I knew then.

'Wycombe is a very fine and very clean market town. The people are looking extremely well: the girls are somewhat larger featured and of larger build than their sisters further south' wrote William Cobbett (1763-1835) in an unusually good mood some 200 years ago.

The 'Wye Coombe', or valley of the Wye, is possibly a derivation of the town's name. About 800AD it is written as 'Wichama'. In pre-Norman days the Lord of the Manor was a Saxon called Brictric, whilst in the Domesday Book the lord was Robert D'Oilly. But the area was settled long before those times. There was a substantial Roman villa alongside the river on what we now call The Rye, which had fourteen rooms, a bath and a 10ft wide gateway, while Desborough Castle, earthworks on West Wycombe Hill and other high points indicate settlements even before Roman times.

In the early Middle ages, King Stephen camped at Desborough Castle and the opposing forces of Queen Mathilda around the earthwork in the grounds of what is now the Castle Hill Museum.

Wycombe's prosperity lay with the River Wye, which must have been swift flowing and possibly wider than today. By 1306, there was a thriving corn grinding and cloth industry. Indeed, it was Wycombe men who manufactured the course cloth for Edward I's army tents. Eventually cloth gave way to the traditional Chiltern crafts of lace-making and straw-plaiting. Paper making became important and by 1600 the industry was flourishing.

Yet Wycombe's industrial fame came in the late eighteenth century, when the manufacture of chairs became industrially organised. By 1890 there were 50 factories and in the next fifty years more companies were founded. Wycombe became the 'Chairmaking Capital of England' and one writer said of the late Victorian town that 'it consists of Chapels, Children and Chairs'. Certainly, non-Conformist chapels and churches became a feature of the town's landscape.

Thomas Ellwood, friend of John Milton and a leader of the Society of Friends in the seventeenth century, was imprisoned in the town. Later, John Wesley visited Wycombe many times. A local lady, Hannah Ball (the site of whose house is marked in Queen's Square) was the pioneer of Sunday Schools in the town. 'She has a peculiar love for children and a talent for assisting them' Wesley wrote of her.

As the nineteenth century got underway, the town became an important centre of the coaching trade on the road to Oxford and inns such as The Red Lion and The Falcon were important stopping places. It was from the balcony of The Red Lion in 1832 that Benjamin Disraeli made an impassioned speech to the electors of the town. He was unsuccessful, but he was to be forever linked with the area when he came to live at Hughenden Manor.

The coach trade came to an end when the Great Western Railway's broad gauge line arrived from Maidenhead in 1854. Subsequently, the line was extended to Princes Risborough, Oxford and Aylesbury. Yet oddly, the furniture trade seems to have been reluctant to use the railway, preferring the old, slow, but direct form of delivery by heavily loaded horse and cart.

In 1906, the new main line from Paddington and Marylebone – the Great Western and Great Central Joint Committee line – was constructed and Wycombe was at last on the main line railway map.

The end of the nineteenth century saw the beginning of many changes. Lord Carrington sold part of the lands of Wycombe Abbey for the municipal centre and Queen Victoria Road was constructed across the site.

The story of Wycombe in the last hundred years is told in this collection of old postcards and photographs. Here you will see places long gone and others that are still recognisable . . . but only just. In these closing years of the century, our country towns are undergoing more changes than ever before and are experiencing the pressures of ever-increasing traffic and the demands for office blocks and out-of-town shopping complexes.

Some local history books are written for local historians; the purpose of this book is to give pleasure and to introduce the visitor and new residents to something of the history and background of the busy town of today.

Dennis Edwards
Uxbridge, July 1997

One

Distant Prospects

The centre of the town as it looked in the early 1920s. Top left is the Wesleyan Methodist Church, with Priory Road coming down to the junction with Church Street and Castle Street. McIroys department store is on the left and in the right hand corner is The Priory. In the foreground is White Hart Street.

The town centre from Bellfield over a century ago and the old single track Wycombe-Risborough Railway. In the distance can be seen the new Wesleyan Church in Priory Road. The foundation stone of the church was laid by Lord Carrington in October 1865.

VIEW FROM TOM BURTS HILL, HIGH WYCOMBE. (4)

The town as it looked in the 1940s, with a view from Tom Birt's Hill. Tom Birt was an eighteenth-century land worker and one day, when he was digging out tree roots on this hill, he discovered a treasure trove. With the proceeds he was able to buy a handsome house that still stands in the High Street.

The view from Tom Birt's Hill about 1910. The Newlands area of the town is in the middle of the picture.

The old Loakes Park football ground and the town before the developments for the relief roads and the Octagon Centre. The large building to the right of the church is the Majestic Cinema - originally opened in 1907. By the time this view was taken, it had been rebuilt and renamed the Odeon. To the right can be seen the London Transport Country Bus depot at the foot of Marlow Hill.

What a different scene this would be today, with almost all the buildings in the middle of this view swept away. But in the distance, Castle Hill is recognisable. Castle Hill House was rebuilt by Robert Nash, who was Town Clerk. It is now the Castle Museum.

The old buildings of St Mary's Street and the old hospital with the football ground, seen from Tom Birt's Hill.

A very early postcard view from the hill, with the buildings of Loakes Manor, which was the Dower House to the Abbey.

The Newlands area and the gas works from Roundabout Woods in about 1923.

13

The War Memorial Hospital, erected in memory of the Wycombe men who fell in the First World War. The hospital was built on land given by the Marquis of Lincolnshire (Lord Shelbourne). The site is now Wycombe General Hospital.

Industrial Wycombe seen from Bellfield in Edwardian days. Steam from a shunting locomotive can be seen to the left, just north of Oxford Road. Hughenden Valley (which even then was becoming built up) lies beyond.

14

Tom Birt's Hill has always been a favourite spot for photographers. This 1930s picture shows St Mary's Street and the now vanished Newlands area. The large building to the left of the church tower is the department store of William McIlroy in Church Street.

The town centre as it was in 1922, with St Mary's Street, which dates back to the fourteenth century. The Guildhall, Market Hall and High Street can also be seen.

HIGH WYCOMBE

AND DISTRICT

claims to be the metropolis of the

Furniture and Chair Making Industry

It is also the home of large and important
PAPER MANUFACTURING MILLS

For the EDUCATION of Boys and Girls it offers

For the Boys—
The Royal Grammar School, founded 1550.

For the Girls—
Wycombe Abbey School, Godstowe preparatory School, The Wycombe High School.

The High Wycombe Higher Education Committee provide a Junior Day Technical School and a School of Industrial Art, Etc., Etc.

The District for RESIDENTIAL PURPOSES has developed and is developing rapidly, comprising the lovely villages of Hazelmere, Totteridge, Tylers Green, Holmer Green, Penn, Flackwell Heath, West Wycombe, Bradenham, Downley, Naphill, Stokenchurch, with their unsurpassable scenery and attractions.

For BOATING, from Bourne End and Marlow down the river to Henley, and up the river to Cookham and Maidenhead, one of the most magnificent stretches of the Thames. At Bourne End is the UPPER THAMES SAILING CLUB.

For GOLF, Flackwell Heath Golf Course, 18 holes.

The Country round is unrivalled for its beautiful woodland scenery.

A 1923 trade advertisement for High Wycombe. Most of the information is still relevant today.

Two
Church and Market

The Proclamation of King George V outside the Guildhall on 16 May 1910.

This is the earliest picture of the town, dating from the middle years of Queen Victoria's reign, with some well-to-do people in the street. A visitor at this time commented on 'the beauty of the Borough: for the houses here exceed in magnificence, most of the buildings in the Borough, for goodness of brick, mortar and other materials'. Rather a convoluted way of saying that the buildings in the Market Place were superior in design and construction to those found in the rest of the town!

Of course, the most historic building in almost any town is the church. The present All Saints dates back to the fifteenth century. But an earlier church was consecrated here in 1087 by the Bishop of Worcester, Wolfstan. At that period, Wycombe was in the vast diocese of Lincoln and Wolfstan had to ask special permission for the consecration.

Parts of the present building go back to 1275 when there was a centrally placed tower. During the reconstruction of 1521/22, the tower was moved to its present position.

The tower was restored by Henry Keen in 1755, when the pinnacles were added. Keen was also architect of the Guildhall. The original architect of the fifteenth-century church was its rector, who was a close friend of Cardinal Wolsey and designed the famous Magdalen Tower in Oxford.

All Saints from Church Street in 1907. Traffic seems to have been of little importance, as the horse and cart are parked in the middle of the road. The Black Dog public house was later demolished when traffic began to build up in the 1920s.

The church underwent further extensive alterations in 1887/89 by Oldrid Scott. The interior was restored in 1873 by the famous architect of London's Law Courts, George Street. The east window of 1872 contains fragments of old Flemish glass.

The corner of Church Street in 1938. In the church yard is a witty epitaph to a lady 'who preferred to be, rather than seem, to be learned'.

Winter time view from the 1950s. At this time, one of the shops on the right was a branch of the famous J. Lyons' tearooms.

The old Watch House (an early Victorian structure) and soldiers during the First World War. The fine iron gates to the church yard were once at the entrance to Wycombe Abbey in St Mary's Street.

Shoppers stroll safely across Church Street. In the distance, Priory Road climbs up the hill under the railway to Priory bridge and the buildings of Priory Road School.

Advertisement for McIlroys, dated about 1930. At this time ladies could purchase a tailored two-piece suit for £3 17s, the change from the transaction coming to them by means of an overhead wire system from the store's central cash office. The site is now occupied by Marks and Spencer.

23

Priory Road, High Wycombe.

W.H.A.
Photo Series. 618.

Looking down Priory Road one can see the twin turrets of the Methodist church at the left. At the bottom of the row of houses, right, is the premises of William McIlroy, opened in 1899. The store was part of a group based at Reading, which, at one time, had branches all over the Thames Valley. The only surviving store today is further west, at Swindon.

Multi-view cards were once very popular, particularly with visitors who wanted to show as much as they could of where they were staying to distant friends. The church, gates, Watch House and Guildhall are all on this card of 1911.

When John Petty (Earl of Sherbourne) became an Alderman in 1755, he conducted the many improvements in the town. It is believed that the first Guildhall was nearer the church than the site we see here.

Every year the Guildhall is the scene for Wycombe's unique Weighing the Mayor ceremony is held. The custom dates back to Elizabethan times. Conducted with much enthusiasm, its purpose is to see if the outgoing mayor has put on any weight during his or her term of office, the implication being that the additional weight has been at the expense of the rate-payers.

The Guildhall arches are believed to echo those of the original building on this site. This is a postcard from the First World War period.

1310   HIGH WYCOMBE. GUILDHALL FROM HIGH STREET

Easy parking outside The Falcon in 1949. The shop in the centre with the white blind was at this time occupied by John Farmer, the shoe chain.

The Guildhall from Church Street in the First World War. The emporium of Richard Dring, draper and outfitter, was founded in 1864 and lasted until fairly recent times.

The Guildhall has a barely readable inscription (even today) which says: 'Erected in the year of our Lord 1752 at the expense of John Earl of Shelbourne in memory of which the Corporation caused this to be written'.

A Sunday morning view of the Guildhall and The Falcon Inn from the Market House. The architect of the Guildhall, Henry Keen, was also architect of the Radcliffe Hospital in Oxford.

Busy shopping day scene in the Market Place about 1955. Dring's drapery and clothing store and John Farmer's shoe shop are in the background.

The Little Market House, which is nowadays usually just known as the Market House. It was designed by the famous Robert Adam in 1761. He was busy at West Wycombe House and perhaps only devoted the minimum amount of time to the Wycombe project – hardly one of his best essays.

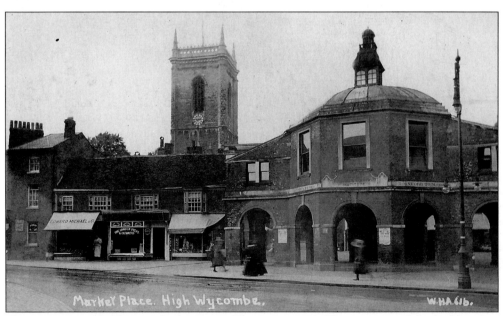

The turret was added later and is known as 'The pepper pot'. The area around the building was originally The Shambles where meat was sold.

Market House and Guildhall in the 1920s. There has been a flourishing market here since at least 1245.

Sir John Stockton left money in 1470 for the construction of a covered market house. In 1766 it is recorded that commodities such as 'fish, butter, geese, chickens, duck, pigeons and rabbits' were sold here.

White Hart Street with the Wycombe branch of the once well-known Home and Colonial Stores on the right.

It is Christmas 1931 and this is the traditional, if unhygenic, display outside Aldridges well-known shop in White Hart Street.

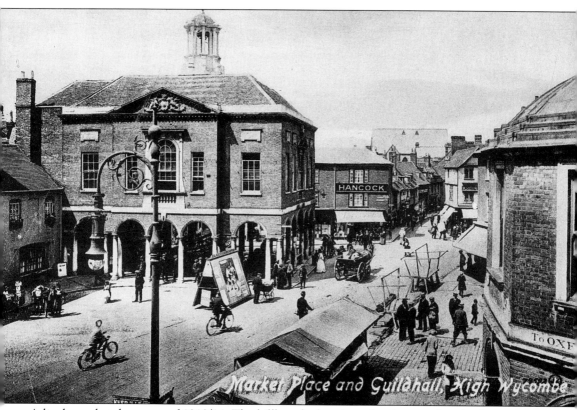

A lively market day scene of 1913/14. The billboard advertises a boxing match to be shown at the Electroscope Cinema of 1912 (which later became the Rex) in Frogmoor.

Here are some 'rated inhabitants of the Borough' on their way back from grazing on the Rye in about 1912. The canopy over the entrance to The Red Lion was where Disraeli gave his famous, if unproductive, election speech in 1832.

Two views of the famous Wycombe Chair arches. This one was erected in 1880 for the visit of Edward and Alexandria, Prince and Princess of Wales. The arch was made up of some 300 chairs.

The 1880 arch seen here is made of a wide variety of chairs then being made in the town. There was a similar arch in 1877, when Queen Victoria passed through the streets on her way to visit Disraeli at Hughenden.

High Street, High Wycombe

The late 1920s and more motor traffic – although what was then the main through route to Oxford hardly looks busy. On the left are the premises of the Conservative Club whose foundation stone was laid on 16 December 1897 by A.J. Balfour MP (and First Lord of the Treasury) in the presence of Coningsby Disraeli and Viscount Curzon.

High Street, 1900, with the Red Lion Hotel. Recorded in 1312, it belonged to Brasenose College, Oxford, and in the heyday of the coaching trade had stables for 42 horses.

Advertisement for The Red Lion, 1923. The hotel had a spacious first floor restaurant that was still flourishing in the 1950s.

The white building on the right is at the corner of the then new Corporation Street and was the premises of the Wycombe Bank (now Lloyds).

The High Street with one of the new gas lamp standards. Gas was supplied to the town by the High Wycombe Gas Light and Coke Company. Buckingham House on the left hand side was known as Bobbin Castle because of its association with the lace making trade.

High Street near the junction with Corporation Street, c. 1912. At one time the council hoped that the post office (then in Easton Street) would be moved there. At the time of this picture, Corporation Street contained few buildings except the Roman Catholic Church of St Augustine, later moved up to Amersham Hill. The shop with the blind is now the premises of Abbey National.

Market day in 1907. The stall holders' rent (or 'dues') were collected in the small room on the octagonal first floor of the Market House.

The 1920s brought the age of the motorist and The Red Lion at this time had passed under the ownership of Trust Houses.

The High Street in 1902. The building nearest the camera (right) was the headquarters of the Liberal association. Next to The Red Lion was The Antelope. Disraeli called here that day in 1832 when he made his speech: 'I jumped up on to the portico of The Red Lion and gave them for an hour and a quarter. I can give you no idea of the effect. I made them all mad. A great many cried. I never made as many friends in my life – or converted as many enemies. All the women on my side and wore my colours – pink and white'.

A 1934 postcard. Shops on the right include Ward's Cafe, the Imperial stores and Barclays Bank.

The age of the car – the High Street 1935/6, with Lees garage on the left, complete with Pratts Petrol pumps and, beyond, The Three Tuns (which dates from 1840).

On to the 1950s. Just beyond The Red Lion are the premises of David Grieg, the multiple grocer. It was on this side of the street in the early nineteenth century that there was an academy for young army officers. It later moved to Sandhurst. In 1945, Winston Churchill made a speech from the top of the Red Lion canopy.

The good old days? One of the narrow alleys of the now vanished Newlands part of the town. The St Paul's Mission is on the right. A survey made towards the end of the Victorian period showed that up to 40 people from this ill-lit and badly constructed place had to share one privy. Clearance of the area began before the Second World War.

Down to the eastern end of High Street near the junction (right) of what was then narrow Crendon Lane. The stone gatehouses and entrance to Wycombe Abbey stood on the left by the fine terrace of eighteenth-century houses. The gates were removed to Marlow Hill ready for the construction of Queen Victoria Street at the end of the nineteenth century.

HIGH WYCOMBE, HIGH STREET.

The sixteenth-century White House is still a landmark in this part of the town. For many years, the building (with its early eighteenth-century frontage) was the premises of Edward Sweetland, the photographer. The shop on the corner was rebuilt when Crendon Street was created out of the old Crendon lane in 1931/2. Behind the White House stood the premises where the Society of Friends (the Quakers) met for many years before they moved to London Road (by the Stuart Road).

Three
Around the Town

Oxford Street, with Frogmoor on the left. The distinctive three-gabled building in the distance was The Hen and Chickens, an ancient inn dating from 1765, but rebuilt in 1888. The ground floor is now occupied by shops.

Frogmore Gardens.

Frogmoor probably derives its name from a patch of marshy ground where the brook from Hughenden came down to meet the Wye. In the seventeenth century, this part of the town, which was then on the outskirts, contained a House of Correction, where the Quaker Thomas Ellwood was imprisoned. In 1734, the Common Council of Wycombe had the space landscaped and a lake (or ornamental 'canal') dug and trees planted.

Frogmoor, seen here (and in the previous picture) at the turn of the century, shows the ornamental fountain installed at the expense of James Griffiths, a wealthy local man and at one time the Recorder for Reading. The gardens opened in April 1877 and the local Militia band played the National Anthem as the first jets of water shot from the fountain.

By 1909, the trees had matured and many of the houses had been converted into shops. J.I. Popp newsagent and tobacconist is on the right.

Summer in Frogmoor, with an ice-cream seller and a lady at what appears to be a charity table. She is talking to a postman.

Frogmore Gardens, High Wycombe.

The Frogmoor fountain became very dilapidated and its ornamental bowl filled with rubbish. During the scrap drive of 1940, the fountain was removed and eventually the trees also went. In the distance can be seen the distinctive building of the Science and Art School.

Science & Art Schools, High Wycombe.   W 8734

The Science and Art School was opened by Lord Carrington on 13 December 1893. In 1929, the building was converted into a swimming bath. After the Second World War, it was a theatre for a short period. Frogmoor House is on the right. In the nineteenth century it was the home of William Gallimore, 'sometime medical official and public vaccinator'. At the time this picture was taken, the house was a girl's school.

Two views of Frogmoor in more recent times. The once leafy gardens have given way to a treeless space. The railway bridge is in the distance, by the Art School. The Palace Cinema has a history dating back to 1909. In its early days, performances were given at 7 pm and 9 pm nightly, 'with high-class vaudeville acts and animated pictures'. Seats at 3d, 6d, 9d 1/-, and matinees every Saturday at 2 pm. The shop next to the cinema is Pilot Luxury Coaches and travel office.

Round the corner into Oxford Street, where today hardly a single building seen in this 1930s picture now exists. The picture may have been taken on a summer Bank Holiday – note the

men in their best suits and caps – near The Half Moon public house. The impressive building with the ornate facade opened as the Electroscope Theatre in 1909.

The area looked very unattractive in this 1950s study. All the buildings on the right have now gone and the site is now occupied by the Chiltern Shopping precinct. The tall building with the half-timbred gable to the far left, is now the showrooms of Parker-Knoll.

Oxford Road, looking towards Oxford Street. On the right is the River Wye and the cottages occupied by workers in the furniture trade. Note the '1d and 6d bazaar' on the left.

Oxford Road in the 1900s, looking west. The cottages on the left were demolished and the River Wye in front of them covered over in the latter half of 1965.

The Oxford Road area was home to a large number of workers in the chair industry, the more affluent living along the road in slightly larger houses. If you examine the right hand side of the picture you can see a housemaid leaning dangerously out of a first floor window over one of the shops, as she industriously cleans the glass.

On one fine day the Councillors
Of Wycombe Town all met,
And said "We must enforce this Law,
For we've done nothing yet."

"To lessen either Rate or Tax
Would surely be a crime,
Let's start with this old musty Law
Of Charles the Second's time."

The newsagent and tobacconist shop of J.I. Popp in Frogmoor was another long established business, lasting until at least the end of the 1950s. The shop was involved in the famous Sunday Trading case in the early 1920s in which the local council cited a law of Charles II that made it illegal to trade in certain goods on Sundays. This is one of a series of humorous cards issued at the time – complete with verse! Between 1901/08 Joseph Popp appeared in court 340 times charged with selling tobacco and postcards on Sunday. He was fined a total of £150, but was re-imbursed by the profits he made from supporters from far and wide who came to his shop to buy goods on a Sunday!

John Busby's shoe shop was in Oxford Street for many years. This advertisement dates from 1922.

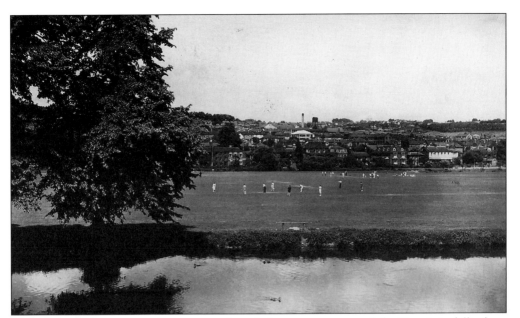

Back through the town to the eastern side and the green expanse of the Rye. It is difficult to imagine this peaceful spot being the site of a battle. But in 1642, a Royalist force under Lord Wentworth marched into the town from Oxford, thinking it would be an easy prize. They were mistaken. An army of Parliamentary forces under Captain Hayes surprized them and there was a fierce fight in which the Royalists lost 900 men and Captain Hayes 300. The only battles fought here today are those of cricket, which has been played here since 1774.

The Boating Lake (or Dyke) was formerly part of the grounds of Wycombe Abbey. The old Windsor Road crossed the edge of the Rye here until the end of the eighteenth century.

For centuries, the Burgesses of Wycombe were each allowed to graze two cows and a heifer during daylight hours on the Rye. The right ended in 1927, when the area was made into a public park.

The Rye, however, has always been open to the citizens of the town. Three hundred years ago a document tells us that 'All the inhabitants of the Borough have liberty at all times to walk and to use sports and pastimes'. The sports included broad sword fighting and football.

The walk along by the Dyke is known as Wendover Way in memory of Viscount Wendover (son of the Marquis of Lincolnshire) who was killed in the First World War. Across the green acres are the two distinctive towers of Holy Trinity United Reformed Church built in 1850.

Winter on the Wye alongside the London Road. In the distance are the buildings of Bassetbury Mill. The Mill and the Manor house take their name from Alan Basset, who owned the buildings in 1203.

The same spot in summer. The children's playground is now sited here. Notice how much wider the Wye was in Edwardian days.

London Road in 1908, with little traffic to bother the inhabitants of the large houses. The house with the verandah nearest the camera is Wick Cottage, with Lynton House and, a little further along, Riverview House with its distinctive turret.

London Road looking east near the junction with Harlow Road. Most of the front garden boundaries are still intact 90 years later!

London Road near Trinity Church and Crown House School. Trinity Church was built in 1850 at a cost of £4000. The achitect was Charles Searle.

The River Wye and the Mill Pond. Pann Mill can just be seen in the distance where London Road becomes Easton Street. Beyond Holy Trinity, are the ruins of the Hospital of St John and the Royal Grammar School, founded here in 1562. At that time, the Master had an annual salary of £8 and the right to graze a cow on the nearby Rye.

The Mill Pond and Pann Mill. There is evidence that there was a mill here in 1185 and it was certainly flourishing in 1235. The name is said to come from Roger de Pani in the thirteenth century. By 1921, the premises were occupied by the Jarvis family.

Pann Mill as it was in the early 1950s. The site was cleared in 1971, but some of the mill machinery was kept there and is now in a museum on the site.

Easton Street was originally Estyntown or East Town. A fair was held here on the Feast of Thomas the Martyr until the sixteenth century. Many of the ancient buildings have gone in the last 30 years. On the left, beyond the shop with the blinds, are the trees in front of the Baptist Chapel of 1845.

ESTD.
1854

ESTD.
1854

DEVONSHIRE DAIRY

Proprietor—H. BUDD

76 EASTON STREET
HIGH WYCOMBE

NEAR POST OFFICE

PURE MILK SUPPLIED DIRECT
FROM LOCAL FARMS

There were almshouses, shops and the post office in Easton Street. This advertisement of seventy-five years ago is for one of the many dairies that were found in the area. At 21 Easton Street was the shop of Money and Co. Cycle and Motor dealers and specialists in talking machines and records.

The old Post Office, Easton Street, in about 1914. The Post Office moved to a splendid new building in Queen Victoria Street in 1934.

62

CRENDON STREET, HIGH WYCOMBE.

H. 1954.

Narrow Crendon Street was transformed in the early 1930s into a street of handsome, if somewhat suburban, buildings. On the left is Norman Reeves' garage and car showrooms, which has now been replaced by Phoenix House. Before the railway was built, the grounds of Castle Hill House came down to Castle Street.

A pleasant summer day in the 1950s, with the Library of 1935 and the Town Hall beyond. The land here was originally part of the grounds of Wycombe Abbey and the main entrance gates and lodge stood here. Lord Carrington sold the land to the town at the beginning of the century.

A very new Queen Victoria Street and the sparkling new Town Hall in 1905. The building was designed by J.J. Bateman and cost £14,000. Arthur J. Dix designed a series of stained glass windows in 1911, depicting the history of the town.

Looking north from the Wye bridge about 1910. The White House and the shops at the corner of what was then Crendon Lane are in the distance.

The Municipal Offices, Queen Victoria Road, by R.G. Brocklehurst and Cowles Vosey, 1932.

Queen Victoria Road late 1940s. In the distance can be seen Crendon Street and the new buildings leading up to the station.

Queen Victoria Road about 1949. In the centre is Crendon Street and the spire of Christ Church, designed by the architect Arthur Veron and built between 1889/97. A guide book called it 'a red brick structure of Early English style'.

The imposing gates to Wycombe Abbey on Marlow Hill. They were removed from High Street (now the site of Queen Victoria Road) in 1897/1901 and re-erected here by Hull, Loosely and Pearce in 1901.

The entrance seen here is probably that to what is now part of The Rye near Pann Mill.

A rural aspect of the grounds of Wycombe Abbey ninety years ago. The estate was originally part of ancient Loakes Manor and of St John's Hospital in Easton Street. At the Reformation, the lands passed to John Cocks who subsequently sold them to John Raunce, who was Mayor of Wycombe in 1552.

The title Abbey was a fashionable one for country houses in the eighteenth century. James Wyatt enlarged and altered the house, following reconstruction work carried out by Henry Keen. Lord Shelbourne sold the estate to a wealthy banker, Robert Smith (later created Lord Carrington).

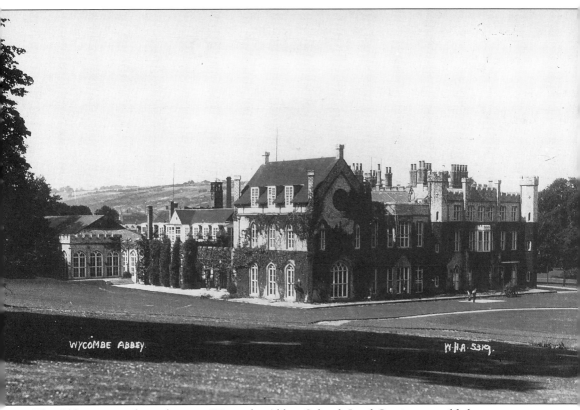

The Abbey, soon after it became Wycombe Abbey School. Lord Carrington sold the estate to the Girls Education Company in 1896 and moved to the more modern Daws Hill House.

Gardening was one of the pastimes encouraged at the Abbey School in Edwardian days.

In the seventeenth century, the estate was owned by John Archdale, and then, in 1700, it passed to Henry Petty. His Irish title was Earl of Shelbourne and he is commemorated in the parish church. His nephew John Fitzmaurice inherited the land, took the name of Petty, and created the title of the Earl of Shelbourne. The view here is of the Abbey soon after it had become the famous school.

By 1905, the school was already one of the most prominent in England. The principal of Clare College, Cambridge, wrote of the school buildings: 'The place is an ideal one for a girls' school. The house is picturesque and possessed of beautiful corridors and large rooms, which, with their fine proportions and old pannelling serve admirably the purpose to which they are now put. I am sure that no girl could spend long in this beautiful place without being influenced for good by her surroundings'.

One of the school houses built between 1898/1909. They were designed by the celebrated architect Caroe, who also designed the Chapel.

In each house, 'every girl lives a carefully ordered home life' said a report of 1924. But during the Second World War, the school moved and the buildings were occupied from 15 May 1942 by the personnel of the United States Army Airforce. Amongst famous visitors was the Glen Miller band.

My dear B...
this is t...
front...
to the...
wri...
to m...
soon
you ha...
yet. an...
cant wri...

Postcard sent from Wycombe Abbey in 1928. The Principal of the School when it opened was Miss Frances Dove, an ardent supporter of the Suffragette Movement. She was elected to the Wycombe Council in 1907. Later, she was elected Mayor, but was not permitted to take up office under the 'male only' rule of that time.

The grounds of Wycombe Abbey were laid out by the famous Capability Brown, who created a lake, grotto and ice-cave. A distant view of the Abbey from the tennis courts, 1911.

On Marlow Hill, 1905, with the boundary walls of the Abbey on the left. The cottage and trees on the right are situated in what is now the centre of this very busy road.

Daws Hill House, Marlow Hill, and the home, from 1896, of Lord Carrington (later Marquis of Lincolnshire). The buildings are now part of the Abbey School.

Across the town now and up past the station to Amersham Hill. Tall and roomy late Victorian houses for the more wealthy professional and business men of the town. On the right is the junction with Totteridge Road. Today, a number of these fine houses have become empty and their windows boarded up.

Godstowe School, Shrubbery Road as it looked in 1910. This postcard was sent to New South Wales, Australia, Christmas 1910 by a teacher at the school. It catered for boys and girls.

Slightly later view from Benjamin's footpath and the cemetery. The school takes its name from the association of the site in ancient times with Godstowe Nunnery in Oxfordshire. In the 1920s, the curriculum included practical courses in bookbinding, carpentry, modelling, gardening, needlework and music. 'The resident scholars are accommodated . . . .in five throroughly up-to-date boarding houses, where every provision is made for the comfort, health and happiness of the pupils.'

No history of Wycombe would be complete without a picture of the furniture trade. This is a very early view of Walter Skull and Sons factory in Oxford Street in about 1880. The family were long associated with the town and Thomas Skull was Town Crier in 1829.

One of the peculiarities of the chair industry was that much of the work was undertaken by domestic-based workers or from small suppliers. The advertisement here appeared in 1922.

Busy scene at the Ercol factory in 1925. The company was founded by Lucien Ercol. Girls were employed in the industry from the age of 12 in Victorian days. Pre-1914 rates of pay would be 23/4d for caning a chair or 6d for a chair with rush seats.

Upholstery section at the Ercol factory in 1925. Today there are about 20 main manufacturers of furniture in the Wycombe area.

Four
Rails and Roads

Rebuilding the railway at Wycombe, *c.* 1902 with workmen and railway officials. There is some mystery about the exact location of this picture. However, one can see the new station building in the course of erection behind the old signal box.

The railway arrived at Wycombe on 1 August 1854 in the form of a Broad Gauge branch line from Maidenhead and Bourne End. The railway was extended through the hills to Princes Risborough and Thame on 1 August 1862 and from Princes Risborough to Aylesbury just over a year later, in October 1863. In October 1870 the lines were narrowed to Standard Gauge and this is what the track looked like just to the west of the town in 1890.

The same spot a few years prior to work beginning on the reconstruction of the railway. The view point is from Bellfield.

The depot for Mackay and Davies of Cardiff, the contractors for the reconstruction of the railway west of Wycombe. New sidings are being laid out and the embankment above Frogmoor is being widened ready for the double track main line.

New double track main lines completed and the sidings almost ready for the first goods trains, autumn 1905. The sidings here closed in 1966 and the site is now mainly occupied by large retail warehouses.

A final view from Bellfield in about 1914, when the new railway was fully operational. Wycombe North signal box, on the left, closed in 1976.

Not the opening of the new line, but the town's welcome to the men of the Buckinghamshire Light Yeomanry home from the South African War, May 1901. Note the old footbridge on the left and the busy goods yards.

Building the new railway from Beaconsfield, near Whitehouse Tunnel. There were several falls of chalk here and six men were killed. The contractor was R.W. Paulin and Company, who were early pioneers in the use of mechanical digging equipment.

The Great Western & Great Central Joint line was built for high speed running on the minimum of gradients. This involved deep cuttings and high embankments. Here a light locomotive – possibly Manning Wardle Number 58 'Beaconsfield' – is tipping material to form the Loudwater embankment.

Looking towards the Wye Valley at Loudwater from the top of the new Whitehouse tunnel, 1904. The work here consisted of several short viaducts and bridges – one specially constructed in red brick at the request of Sir Philip Rose of Rayners.

Construction work west of the station, by the Priory Road and Frogmoor bridges. The tower of the Art School is on the left.

Track widening near Gordon Road, with the premises of the High Wycombe Steam Laundry Company on the right.

Amersham Hill bridge just west of the station, with sections of the old style Great Western track. Just through the bridge can be seen the old station footbridge and the new retaining wall which was built using more than a million blue Staffordshire bricks.

Special train bringing guests of the Great Central Railway to the opening ceremonies at Wycombe on 2 April 1906. There was a grand luncheon at the new Town Hall sponsored by the Chamber of Commerce and guests were entertained between speeches by the organ (which came from the old St James Concert Hall in Piccadilly) played by S.M.A. Galpin. 'The new railway has been constructed with an eye to the future', said one of the speakers. At last, Wycombe was on the main line railway map.

The new station with its curiously shaped chimneys. The posters advertise excursion fares on the new line. The final section of the railway was opened between Bicester and Aynho Junction (south of Banbury) on 4 April 1910 (for goods trains) and on 1 July 1910 for passengers.

Poster advertising the new fast services, which were rivalled by those operated from Euston by the London and North Western Railway via Rugby. It was now possible to travel from Wycombe to Birmingham Snow Hill in about an hour and a half.

The last years of steam; a Birmingham-bound express rushes through on the fast line. The locomotive is 'Star' Class, Number 4061 'Glastonbury Abbey'. This picture is taken from the 'up' platform in June 1959.

This advertising newspaper looks almost modern, yet it was issued in 1910 and distributed at Wycombe station. For all the expense of building the line (estimated at £4000 per mile) the railway was never really profitable, particularly with goods services. But local trains soon began to bring what we now term commuters. A travel guide book announced: 'from early morning to late at night no hour passes without its train'.

A railway oddity - two London bound trains alongside each other just west of the footbridge from Priory Avenue to Castle Street in 1959. The reason was engineering work in the station area. The train on the left is for Paddington, with 'Hall' Class Number 4941. 'LLangedwyn Hall' on the right is a local for Marylebone.

Parcels train approaching the footbridge in July 1959. The rather dirty locomotive is an ex-LMS Stanier 'Black Five'. The signal box was demolished nearly 20 years ago.

West Wycombe station was actually alongside the West Wycombe Road and more convenient for the suburbs of High Wycombe than the famous village. Here a Paddington-bound train is coming around the sharp curve with 'Hall' Class locomotive, Number 5927 'Guildhall' in October 1956.

View of the railway and main Oxford road from West Wycombe Hill, late 1930s. Much of the open land here has now been 'improved' with housing estates. West Wycombe station can just be seen by the cutting. The station closed on 3 November 1958, the goods yards lasting until March 1963. A public house near the site of the old yard is called 'The Friend at Hand' and shows a GWR porter helping a Victorian passenger.

Digging deep with steam excavation equipment near Saunderton in 1903/4. A group of local children watch from the rim of the cutting. The surveyors wanted to ensure that the new high speed railway had no gradient steeper than 1 in 164. A short tunnel was built along this stretch, which is in a 65ft deep cutting.

Work was not easy – here gangs of men are roped together as they carry out finishing work on the Saunderton cutting. The line here is single as it is the 'up' track; the 'down' line uses the route of the original Wycombe-Princes Risborough railway.

Fifty years later and a British Railways express for Paddington speeds through the cutting with an unidentified 'Castle' class locomotive.

Saunderton station July 1957 and a 'King' Class locomotive Number 6005 'King George II' pauses at the platform because of delays caused by engineering work. Part of West Wycombe hill can be seen on the right.

Racing through the Chilterns in 1938, at the point (on the left) where the separate 'up' line rejoins the 'down' line 'King' Class locomotive Number 6008, 'King James II'.

To the roads now and the centre of Wycombe outside The Falcon. The year is 1901 and the coach is actually on a special run for coaching enthusiasts.

At The White Blackbird, Loudwater, 1913. This is the last day of the old horse bus service that ran right through Wycombe and terminated at The Swan in West Wycombe. The driver is Mr Axton of Farnham Common. The operators were The Livery and Posting Company. The fare cost 3d. The production of 'The Yeomen of the Guard' was at Guildhall.

The western end of the horse bus route – The Swan at West Wycombe. A two-horse, 24 seater bus in 1903. The service was often delayed by herds of cattle in the middle of Wycombe, as well as market day traffic. In 1892, there were proposals for a steam tramway from West Wycombe to Loudwater. In 1907, a motor bus service was operated, although there were official criticisms on the 'advisability of running motor buses through the streets of the town'.

Early motoring days were fraught with mechanical breakdowns and driving mishaps on badly maintained roads. This accident took place just outside West Wycombe on the junction of the Oxford Road and the road to Bledlow.

Early motor journeys were made on roads that to us seem uncannily empty. A view of West Wycombe from the Pedestal in about 1914.

After the First World War, organised tours of the Chilterns were popular. Here, two open top coaches separated by London General Country Buses pause in the Market place whilst the drivers shatter the peaceful afternoon with their commentary delivered through tin megaphones.

The same street in the 1950s. A Thames Valley 'Bristol' type bus waits outside The Falcon. The Thames Valley Bus Company began operation on 10 July 1920, taking over earlier established local bus routes. A bus garage was built at Wycombe Marsh in 1924. The Company amalgamated with the Aldershot and District Bus Company in 1971 and the garage closed when the present bus station and garage opened in the 1970s at The Octagon.

Once a familiar sight at Frogmoor. Service 25 'Bristol' type bus for Flackwell Heath, with an older type bus behind.

Horse drawn transport for chairs. Benjamin North, who lived in West Wycombe, wrote the lines:

'Twas the month of May   When with our horse and cart,
From Wycombe we did start,   We left our home to do our best
And Monday was the day   And with the Lord we left the rest.'

In March 1904, William Keen of Desborough Road decided to experiment with a novel form of road traction. The local press reported that 'A novelty in the transport of chairs from Wycombe to London has been introduced this week . . . the motor is capable of drawing six tons'. Apparently, 700 chairs could be hauled – but the return trip took 14 hours.

Five

West Wycombe

Before Sir Francis Dashwood build West Wycombe Road, Desborough Road was the main route to Stockenchurch and Oxford. Note the furniture makers wood yard on the left, with crane to lift the heavy beech tree trunks.

The Pedestal, West Wycombe.

W.H.A.
Photo Series. No 88

Looking towards West Wycombe Hill on a rainy day in 1909. In the distance, the horse bus is about to leave the village street on its route to Wycombe and Loudwater.

The Pedestal was erected in 1752 to commemorate the completion of the new road to Wycombe. It is rather curiously inscribed: From the University – from the City – from the County Town (Oxford, London and Aylesbury).

By the 1930s the Pedestal was on an island at the junction of the Oxford and Aylesbury Roads.

A fine view of the long straight of the Oxford Road from West Wycombe Hill, with the Mausoleum. The original main road ran along the Wye Valley (right). The 1st Earl of Dashwood constructed the present road using chalk excavated from West Wycombe caves.

The hill with the Mausoleum and the distinctive golden ball on the top of the church on a summer day in about 1952.

The Pedestal in the late 1940s with commercial traffic coming along the main road. The Pedestal is now at the side of the road and there is a mini-roundabout here.

The church and Mausoleum were created by Lord le Despencer (Sir Francis Nashwood) in 1763/4.

The Mausoleum was intended to be a resting place for the departed members of the Dashwood family. The money for its construction was left by a close friend, George Dudington of Melcombe Regis in Dorset.

The Mausoleum is eight sided and contains memorials, some of which come from the church. There is an urn and a pedestal monument to Lady le Despencer, dated 1769. The architect of the Mausoleum was John Bastard the younger, of Blandford.

Church Loft, West Wycombe

The village passed from the Dashwoods to the Royal Society of Arts in 1929 – despite some local opposition. The village eventually became the property of the National Trust. Church Loft dates from the fifteenth century, but the bell turret is seventeenth-century.

The main street of West Wycombe in 1903, with the Church Loft on the right. In the distance (on the left) is the Swan Inn and the horse bus waiting to depart for the more everyday surroundings of Wycombe.

A well-known view in West Wycombe – the Church Loft from Church Lane. For centuries the local Vestry met in the ancient building. In 1721 it was recorded that money was to be allocated 'for cleaning the Widow Plumridge of lice.'

The tower of St Lawrence dates from the fourteenth century, but the main body of the building was transformed by the 2nd Earl Dashwood. The golden ball on top of the tower is said to have been based on that at the Custom House in Venice, which the Earl had admired on the Grand Tour.

There is a legend that members of the Hell Fire Club sometimes met in the golden ball. Certainly, Dashwood entertained his friends there. John Wilkes wrote, following a visit in 1762 with Charles Churchill, that they drank 'divine milk punch and sang jolly songs very unfit for the profane ears of the world below'. He also records that it was 'the best Globe Tavern I was ever in'.

St Lawrence stands on the site of an earlier structure, which was in the vanished village of Haverington. The settlement was mentioned in the Domesday Book. It eventually moved down the road to Oxford, which became busier in later centuries. Another factor was probably better water supplies. In 1875 West Wycombe had its own parish church – St Paul's, which saved churchgoers the heavy climb up the hill.

'Some churches have been built for devotion; others from parade or vanity. I belive this is the first church which has been built for a prospect'. The unusual interior of the church in 1950.

A visitor in 1775 called the interior 'A very superb Egyption hall'. The fresco work was by Giovanni Bergnis. His father, Guiseppe, who died in 1761, is buried in the churchyard. Both artists were employed in the decorative work on West Wycombe House. One of the monuments in the chancel is to Charles Dashwood (brother of Francis) who was 'cut off in Paris in the flower of his youth and the twenty third year of his age.'

'Is this a mart where gossips sell and buy?
A room for lectures, or a stock exchange?
Is that, which seems a pulpit to the eye,
A desk where auctioneers their labour ply?'

When this picture was taken some forty years ago, it was still possible for visitors to make the hazardous climb up into the golden ball. At one time there was a small stable near the church tower so that the tired horses and worshippers could rest during the service. Charles Churchill wrote about the church in the eighteenth century that it was 'a temple built aloft in air/ That serves for show and not for prayer'.

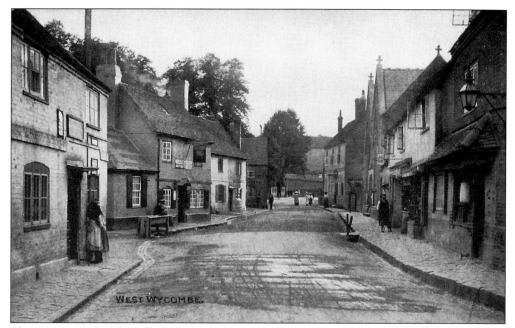

The western end of the village street, with the Methodist Church of 1894 on the right – one of the few buildings whose architecture is somewhat out of keeping with the earlier style. At one time in the 1920s, a rich American offered to dismantle the village and ship it to the States.

Going about their daily work, villagers in this 1900 view hardly realised that their village was even then a rare survivor of a vanished age.

The village from the church tower. West Wycombe Park, to the right, was given to the National Trust in 1944 by Sir John Dashwood.

The perfect village: West Wycombe as it looked in 1937. Since those days, the suburbs of Wycombe have advanced almost to the edge of the parklands.

The river and the two eighteenth-century pavilions known as 'The Pepper Pots' seen in September 1907. Many of the features in the park at West Wycombe House were the work of Nicholas Revett.

Can this really be today's busy A40? With the coming of the railways, the old coach roads became very quiet at times. This is a view towards Stokenchurch, dated 1907.

By the late 1930s, the road had been greatly improved. The lane in the left distance runs up from the road towards Wheeler End Common.

Multi-view card of about 1935 showing the attractions of West Wycombe. By this period, regular bus services and coach trips brought hundreds out to sample the view and marvel at the old buildings and there were traffic jams on Bank Holidays.

Six
Around Wycombe

Cressex Road estate developments in 1934. One local builder advertised: 'Here you can get a freehold detached house for £450 . . . homes built to purchaser's own specification.'

Wycombe Marsh Mill and watercress beds. The cress was at one time grown along almost any local watercourse in the area. The Mill produced paper from about 1720 and at one time had a contract to supply high quality paper to the Civil Service. Until 1896, the Mill was part of the Abbey estate.

Back lane connected a number of mills along the Wye-Bassetsbury, Marsh Green and Wycombe Marsh. The parish Workhouse was also sited nearby. Here is the foot bridge and ford in 1914.

Keep Hill and Deangarden Wood. The busy M40 Motorway now runs along the lower slopes and the area is now a nature reserve.

Flackwell Heath and the Green Man, near the junction with Common Road. All the trees to the right have gone for road widening and the Community Centre and shops occupy the site. But the inn is still recognisable today.

Flackwell Heath and the Three Horse Shoes public house, with Virginia Cottages on the right.

The then-new Christ Church, Flackwell Heath, built in the 1930s for the increased growth of this ridge-top village.

The golf club with the Club House as it looked in about 1932. A guide book of that period described the 18-hole course as having 'hazards of a sporting nature' and as being convenient for Loudwater Station on the Bourne End line.

THE GOLF COURSE, FLACKWELL HEATH.

The fees in about 1929 were: 2/6d and 5/ a day; 18/- per week; and £2 per month. Play 'was permitted on Sundays'.

The Wye Valley and Loudwater from the Golf Course in 1930. The main line railway and the viaduct is in the distance and, to the right, the lane climbs up to Tylers Green.

Typical estate agent's advertisement of the 1920s. The railway fares to London were fairly expensive, though. A monthly third class return to Marylebone cost 6/8d, but there was a day return for 4/9d.

South Buckinghamshire
for
SCENERY & HEALTH

Printed List of Available
Properties on application to

HAROLD J. NUTT

Auctioneer, Property Specialist,
HIGH WYCOMBE

And at GERRARDS CROSS
and BEACONSFIELD.

Please quote Hy. C.C.
when applying

Despite economic depression, a number of new industries came to Wycombe in the inter-war years and the town began to expand. This is the road on the then-uncompleted Desborough estate in the mid-1930s. Local builders of the period included White Brothers on the Copyground Building estate and J. Broad and Son, 'Houses built to Purchaser's requirements'.

The growing suburb of Terriers about 1939. The church was designed by Sir Giles Scott and was consecrated in 1930.

Over to Hazelmere and a view of about 1948, with the Holy Trinity Church of 1845. A new chancel was added in 1958.

Amersham Road, Hazlemere, just after the Second World War. In the last twenty-five years, the area has expanded in all directions with housing developments.

Church Road, Tyler's Green, with the Horse and Jockey. Before the church was built in 1854, the road was called Gomm's Lane. In 1796, Edmund Burke set up a school at Tyler's Green for sixty young French aristocrats who had lost fathers or relations in the French Revolution.

Penn village as seen from the gates of Rayners. This extensive estate was the home of Sir Philip Rayner (1816-1883). He was a political agent for the Conservative Party between 1853/72 and High Sheriff of Buckinghamshire in 1878, as well as being the executor of the Will of Lord Beaconsfield (Disraeli). The house is now an educational establishment.

A rural scene at Four Ashes near Widmer End and Cryer's Hill, 1910.

Bradenham Manor dates from 1670. In the early nineteenth century it became the home of the Disraeli family. Isaac (the father of Benjamin) wrote in 1829 that they were leaving London behind owing to 'the precarious health of several members of my family.' The future great prime minister spent much of his youth here and the house features as 'Hurstley' in his novel *Endymion*.

Wycombe Court is now the site of the Euro-Japanese Study Conference Centre.

Wycombe Court, Lane End, 1937. The writer of this postcard was on a course there and was sending news to an address in Apeldorn, Holland.

Acknowledgements

The majority of pictures are from the author's postcard collection, with supplements by Buckinghamshire County Reference Library, the Wycombe Museum and the late A. Fleming.